Can You
TRUST
Me?

BYRD BAGGETT

TRUE GROWTH

Copyright © 2009 by Byrd Baggett
Published by
True Growth™ Publishing
505 Barrywood Drive, Nashville, TN 37220

Book design by
Bruce Gore | Gore Studio, Inc.
Nashville, TN

Library of Congress Cataloging-in-Publication Data is available
ISBN: 978-1-48205-568-9

Printed in the United States of America

Introduction

The seed for this book was planted during the summer of 1985, while I was on family vacation in Austin, Texas. We were visiting with my parents at their home on beautiful Lake Travis, when a powerful and timely life-changing conversation transpired. My wife, Jeanne, and two children, Amy and Ashley, were out on the lake enjoying all the water activities with my dad. I had stayed back at the house with my mom so that we could share some time alone. Mom was quite ill with a congestive heart disease. She and I were sitting under a majestic oak tree talking about life when she started questioning me about my integrity as a husband. I responded to her, "But, Mom, I'm a good husband." I can still see and feel Mom's eyes as she said, "Son, there are a lot of good people in hell." My mom passed away two months after we had that conversation.

This powerful experience is the story behind one of my favorite quotes in this book: "The truth may sometimes hurt, but it will always help." Mom understood that living the truth was the only way to achieve true success in life, and her honesty ultimately changed my life. Her courage to speak the truth helped me to understand that integrity and truth are inseparable. Quite simply, integrity is the truth and is the ultimate test by which to measure one's character. Thanks, Mom, for holding me to the highest ideal of life.

On another occasion I was having a discussion with one of my clients, interviewing him concerning the topics he wanted me to cover in an upcoming talk I was going to give to his sales team. He singled out integrity as one of the areas he wanted me to emphasize in my presentation. This client then went on to tell me about one of his peers, an executive in charge of another manufacturing division. This senior manager and two sales representatives were making a sales call on a long-term client. It was a relationship that had accounted for most of the division's sales volume. After that meeting was over, the executive noticed that one of their competitor's new product samples had been left behind for the client to evaluate. Thinking they were alone in the room, the executive placed the sample in his briefcase, closed it, and took the sample home to evaluate.

It turns out, however, that the executive and his two sales reps had not been alone in the room. One of the client's representatives had walked back into the room unnoticed and seen the executive swipe the sample. As a consequence of this lack of integrity, both sales representatives were fired and the executive was barred for life from calling on this customer. Millions of dollars in business and a long-term relationship were lost because of one bad error in judgment! This sad but true story is the basis for another of my favorite quotes in this book: "Trust, once lost, is almost impossible to regain."

As these stories illustrate, integrity is the foundation for true success in both our personal and professional lives. A life fulfilled is wisdom lived, not knowledge learned. My single goal for this book is that it serve as a guide as you strive to live a life based on truth. Your journey will not be easy, and your choices may not be popular, but your steadfast commitment to the purity of truth will separate you from the mass of mediocrity. Always search for the truth and never compromise, and the richest blessings of life will be yours!

Can You
TRUST
Me?

TRUTH
IS THE LIFEBLOOD
OF GROWTH.

THE OAK TREE is a great metaphor for life. Like our life, the oak requires moisture to grow. The moisture of life is the truth. As long as we are vulnerable and open to absorbing the truth, we remain vibrant and are able to withstand the inevitable storms of life. Once we cut ourselves off to truth, we become hardened and brittle. Like the oak without water, the challenges of life will slowly but surely break us apart, leaving us a shell of what we could have become if we had only been open to absorbing the truth.

To determine your current season, take the free Readiness for Change assessment at www.truegrowthassociates.com.

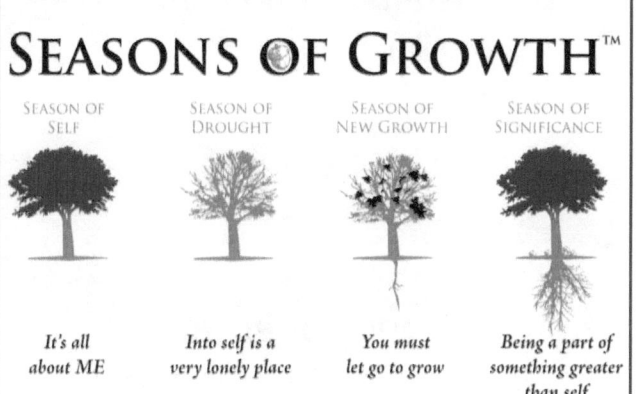

SEASONS OF GROWTH™

SEASON OF SELF	SEASON OF DROUGHT	SEASON OF NEW GROWTH	SEASON OF SIGNIFICANCE
It's all about ME	*Into self is a very lonely place*	*You must let go to grow*	*Being a part of something greater than self*

Practice
what you preach.

Success at the
expense of faith and family
is really failure.

Do the right thing–
always!

Your choice:
the courage of truth
or the cowardice
of compromise.

Once trust is broken,
confidence no longer exists.

TRUTH
Seek it • Speak it •
Expect it • Respect it •
Live it

COMMUNICATION IS THE LIFEBLOOD OF TRUST.

An apology
is a sign of a secure person.

Choose to associate
with those who reflect
your values.

"The truth
is incontrovertible,
malice may attack it,
ignorance may deride it;
but in the end, there it is."
–*Winston Churchill*

The truth
may sometimes hurt,
but it will always help.

$\mathscr{P}$EOPLE
DON'T CARE HOW
MUCH YOU KNOW
UNTIL THEY KNOW
HOW MUCH
YOU CARE.

Personal compromise ultimately leads to professional compromise.

"Truth has no special time of its own. Its hour is now—always."
–*Albert Schweitzer*

People hear what you say,
but they see what you do;
and seeing is believing.

If you don't stand
for something, you will fall for
almost anything.

*C*HOOSE
THE PURITY OF
TRUTH OVER
POPULARITY.

The true test of character
is what one thinks, says, or does
when no one is watching.

Humility is a
constant companion
of integrity.

Watch your thoughts,
because they become
your words.

Watch your words,
because they become
your actions.

Watch your actions,
because they become
your habits.

Watch your habits,
because they become
your character.

Watch your character,
because it becomes
your destiny.

Follow the truth,
not the opinions of others.

It is much easier
to live with the truth than
to suffer with a lie.

"Any man can work when every stroke of his hand brings down the fruit rattling to the ground; but to labor in season and out of season, under every discouragement, by the power of truth… that requires a heroism that is transcendent."

–Henry Ward Beecher

Choose wisdom
over knowledge.

The truth always hurts less
than holding onto a lie.

Arrogance is deadly!

TRUE WISDOM IS NOT A FAD.

What is popular
is not always right, and what
is right is not always popular.

Choose to follow
those you know are on
the right path.

"It is not the number of books you read, nor the variety of sermons you hear, not the amount of religious conversation in which you mix, but it is the frequency and earnestness with which you meditate on these things till the truth becomes your own and part of your being, that ensures your growth."

–*Frederick Robertson*

True success
is always built on a bedrock
of integrity.

It is very important
that you like yourself.

"Truth is tough.
It will not break, like a bubble,
at a touch. Nay, you may kick it
about all day, and it will be
round and full at evening."
–Oliver Wendell Holmes, Sr.

Seek advice from wise counsel.

"THE SOFTEST PILLOW IS A CLEAR CONSCIENCE."

–Dr. Norman Vincent Peale

Never take advantage
of others for personal gain.

The greatest satisfactions
in life come as a result of
living the truth.

Learn from your mistakes,
and don't repeat them!

Stand for something!

Ego: **E**dging **G**od **O**ut

Make it a point to
speak to everyone you meet
as peers, not peons.

Cynicism tempts a compromise of your character– don't give in!

You have a choice between developing good habits and developing bad habits.

Take an active role
in helping your community.

Run from temptation!

Heroes build up;
cowards beat up.

$\mathscr{A}$CTS OF
SELF-SATISFACTION
OFTEN LEAD TO
SELF-DESTRUCTION.

Participate in a
fellowship group. It can be a
great sounding board for any
inner conflict regarding
your values.

Small acts of compromise
ultimately destroy one's character.

Integrity is:
Doing what you
said you would do,
When you said
you would do it, and
How you said
you would do it.

What is buried
within your heart will devour
and destroy you from within.

Bad company
corrupts good morals.

*I*NTEGRITY
IS NEVER
COMPROMISING
THE TRUTH IN
THE MIDST OF
ADVERSITY.

The quality of our life
is determined by the choices
we make.

Focus first on
doing the right things,
not doing things right.

Trust is the lifeblood
of relationships.

Ego: **E**dging **G**rowth **O**ut

"The ultimate test of what a
truth means is the conduct it
dictates or inspires."
–*William James*

If you get to
where you're going,
will you be where you
want to be?

True success
is being at peace with
who you are.

Give others the freedom
to be themselves.

Tell the truth!

Life's greatest battle is
the one within yourself.

Know beforehand
what your proper response will be
to any situation involving
a moral choice.

Seek sincerity, not flattery.

"**E**veryone stumbles over
the truth from time to time,
but most people pick
themselves up and hurry off as
though nothing ever happened."

–Sir Winston Churchill

"**A**s scarce as truth is,
the supply has always been
in excess of the demand."

–Josh Billings

Putting ethics into practice
involves courage more
than conviction.

Spend as much time
developing your character as
you do your personality.

CHARACTER IS MORE IMPORTANT THAN COMPETENCE.

Uncertainty or doubt
is a red flag for any action,
planned or already completed.

Do not
lower your standards to
accommodate others.

We are what we watch,
listen to, and read.

Choose what is right
instead of what is
politically correct.

Always consult
your conscience before
making decisions.

Stand tall through it all.

Success occurs where
dignity and respect abound.

The abuse of power
and people will eventually
result in failure.

Inventory your preferences
of movies, TV shows, music,
and reading material, and remove
the junk from your life!

*L*ISTEN
TO YOUR HEART
AS MUCH AS YOU
DO YOUR HEAD.

A true test of your character: Do you remain the same under intense pressure?

Review the
Ten Commandments,
memorize them,
and live them.

Addictive behavior
can lead to short-term success
but long-term destruction.

If your mind says yes,
but your heart says no, don't!

"**I**t's not the honors and the prizes and the fancy outsides of life that ultimately nourish our souls. It's the knowing that we can be trusted, that we never have to fear the truth, that the bedrock of our very being is firm."

–*Fred Rogers,*
Mister Rogers' Neighborhood

Where we spend
our time and money is a direct
reflection of our priorities.

Responsibility goes
with the territory for those
in positions of authority.

Honor God in all
that you do.

Open communication
thrives in an environment
of total trust.

Trust takes months to earn
but minutes to lose.

Do those closest to you respect you?

Fame at the price of integrity is worthless.

People of integrity are sensitive to others' hearts and souls.

A LIFE
OF INTEGRITY
PROVIDES A CLEAR
SENSE OF PURPOSE
AND MISSION.

Everyone is comfortable
with a person of integrity.

Surround yourself
with those who tell the truth
and not necessarily what
you want to hear.

Relationships Health Quiz

The quality of your life is a direct reflection of the quality of your relationships. Answer the following questions to determine the health of your relationships with friends, family members, and business associates:

1. Do you enjoy being with them?
2. Do you trust them?
3. Do you feel comfortable sharing your feelings with them without fear of retribution?
4. Do they listen without judging or offering advice?
5. Do they tell you what you need to hear, not necessarily what you want to hear?
6 Has the relationship with them improved the quality of your life?
7. Do they drain or energize your spirit?
8. Do you feel better after spending time with them?

Thoughts to ponder:
• How healthy are your relationships?
• What changes do you need to make?

The downfall begins with
justification and rationalization.

It is very important to have
spiritual mentors.

Are you at peace with
your life's direction?

People of integrity find fulfillment in life.

Always have time for the important over the urgent.

"First things first and last things not at all."
–*Peter Drucker*

"He that would
make real progress in
knowledge must dedicate
his age as well as youth,
the latter growth as well
as the first fruits,
at the altar of truth."

–George Berkeley

Passing the buck means
handing over your integrity.

"Till I die, I will not
deny my integrity."
–Job 27:5

Integrity is more important than facts, education, money, appearance, giftedness, or skill.

Those who brag about their honesty should be watched closely.

Into self is a very lonely place.

"*H*ONESTY IS
THE FIRST CHAPTER
IN THE BOOK OF
WISDOM."

–*Thomas Jefferson*

The greatest gift
we can leave our children is a
legacy of integrity.

Integrity is the foundation
of all lasting relationships.

Trust is earned, never acquired.

An environment of trust
creates exceptional results.

The truth never
goes out of style.

Integrity is consistently honoring
commitments and promises.

Show me your friends
and I'll show you your future.

If you burn the
bridges of the past,
you'd better be able to
walk on water.

The higher a person climbs in an organization, the greater is his or her responsibility for living a life of character.

Those of integrity never have to worry about their memory because they always tell the truth.

Honesty will
always be the difference between
winners and losers.

"**T**he only relationships
in this world that have ever been
worthwhile and enduring have
been those in which one person
could trust another."
–*Samuel Smiles*

Integrity can make a company, church, or home; lack of it can break those institutions.

"When regard for truth has been broken down or even slightly weakened, all things will remain doubtful."
–*Saint Augustine*

People of integrity
never run scared.

Confession is
good for the soul,
but only when it's genuine.

It takes much less effort
to tell the truth.

"INTEGRITY IS
THE GLUE THAT
HOLDS OUR WAY OF
LIFE TOGETHER."

–*Billy Graham*

Personal dishonor is the
tragic result of dishonesty.

Truth will win in the end.

Are we living the role
we should be modeling?

Living a life of integrity
makes it easier to
sleep at night.

Integrity has nothing to do
with wealth, knowledge,
or position.

*D*O YOU RESPECT THE FACE IN YOUR MIRROR?

A life of dishonesty
starts with "little white lies."

You can run from the truth,
but you can never hide from it.

Integrity and virtue are
the roots of life.

"Real integrity
stays in place whether the test
is adversity or prosperity."
–*Charles Swindoll*

Live a life of integrity.
Otherwise, the first breeze of
adversity will blow
you away.

A
PERSISTENT LIE: THE END JUSTIFIES THE MEANS.

A loss of integrity involving a "trivial" matter invokes no less a loss of credibility.

Admitting that you were wrong is a lot less painful than covering it up.

"Success in any relationship or endeavor begins with trust."
–*S. Truett Cathy, Founder, Chick-fil-A*®

It is possible to be right
and righteous.

Abide by the decision from
your heart and not the confusion
in your head.

Ask yourself:
What would God do if He were
in my shoes?

"The shadow of
a single man will determine the
destiny of an entire business."
–*Ralph Waldo Emerson*

Those who talk too much
should be watched closely.

THOSE WHO
WALK IN INTEGRITY
ARE CLOTHED IN
HUMILITY.

Integrity is the truth
spoken in love.

Be tolerant, but not indifferent.

Actions always
speak louder than words.

All are entitled to
their opinion, but none are entitled
to their version of the truth.

Bully pulpits don't exist for
men and women of integrity.

"Integrity is never being
ashamed of your reflection."
–*David Cottrell*

FAME IS A VAPOR, POPULARITY AN ACCIDENT, AND RICHES TAKE WINGS. ONLY ONE THING ENDURES AND THAT IS CHARACTER.

– Horace Greeley

Expect people to perform only
as well as the example you set.

Trust your gut feeling;
it's usually right.

True sincerity is a rare
but valuable leadership trait.

Give others the freedom
to make mistakes, and be willing
to forgive them.

Listen with compassion.

Accept blame
as well as fame.

*W*ISDOM IS KNOWING THAT OTHERS MIGHT BE RIGHT.

Those of integrity
can walk with kings without
compromising their virtue.

A strong moral character
is more powerful than
physical strength.

"The love of truth is the stimulus to all noble conversation. This is the root of all the charities. The tree which springs from it may have a thousand branches, but they will all bear a golden and generous fruitage."

–Orville Dewey

True strength
resides in meekness.

When choosing sides,
select those seeking the truth.

Doing what is right
is not an occasional thing,
it's an everyday thing.

Know the difference
between a quick decision
and a rash one.

FIVE STEPS TO BETTER DECISION MAKING

1. **Stop.** Too often we get caught up in the hairball of life and don't stop long enough to reflect on the effectiveness of our decision-making.
2. **Ask the right questions from the right people.** The right people are those who tell you what you need to hear, not necessarily what you want to hear.
3. **Listen objectively with an open mind.** If you don't, you will never get honest feedback again.
4. **Think about the consequences of your choices.** Stop, listen, and think *before* you respond.
5. **Respond** appropriately.

$\mathcal{T}$RUE FREEDOM
COMES AS WE LIVE
THE TRUTH.

Give others a
safe forum to tell you
the truth without retribution.

The proper use of power
should be to influence,
not to control.

We must have the courage
to speak and hear the truth.

"Instruction is what we say.
Influence is what we do.
Image is who we are."
–*Truett Cathy, Founder, Chick-fil-A®*

WE MUST
ULTIMATELY
FACE THE
CONSEQUENCES
OF OUR
CHOICES.

"Give me some men who
are stout-hearted men,
Who will fight for the
rights they adore.
Start me with ten who
are stout-hearted men,
And I'll soon give you
ten thousand more."

–"Stout-Hearted Men,"
Oscar Hammerstein and Sigmund Romberg,
Warner Publishing, 1925

In the words of
Abraham Lincoln:

"The fact is, truth is your
truest friend, no matter
what the circumstances are."
"Let none falter who
thinks he is right."

*I*NTEGRITY
IS A CHOICE.
CHOOSE WISELY.

The following words—written by an Anglican bishop in the 11th century— were found in the crypts of Westminster Abbey...

"When I was young and free my imagination had no limits, I dreamed of changing the world. As I grew older and wiser, I discovered the world would not change, so I shortened my sights somewhat and decided to change only my country. But it, too, seemed immovable. As I grew in my twilight years, in one last desperate attempt, I settled for changing only my family, those closest to me, but alas, they would have none of it. And now as I lie on my deathbed, I suddenly realized: If I had only changed my self first, then by example

I would have changed my family. From their inspiration and encouragement, I would then have been able to better my country and, who knows, I may have even changed my world."

Looking in the mirror of truth is good advice. One of the basic truths in life: The only one you can change is you and by changing yourself, you have the greatest impact on others. Quit trying to "fix" others and work on being the best you can be. It requires the least amount of energy and is the most cost effective investment that you will ever make.

May the **true** riches of life be yours!

OTHER BOOKS BY BYRD BAGGETT

The Book of Excellence

Satisfaction Guaranteed

Taking Charge

Dare to Lead

Power Serve

The Complete Book of Business Success

The Pocket Power Book of Performance

The Pocket Power Book of Leadership

The Pocket Power Book of Motivation

The Pocket Power Book of Integrity

Dare to Soar

The Soul of Winning

The Past Doesn't Have a Future, But You Do

TRUE GROWTH™

The natural choice in leader development

Our mission is to help individuals embrace the transformational power of authenticity to improve themselves and the lives they touch

OUR CORE VALUES

www.growingwinners.com

TRUE GROWTH MODEL™
The natural choice in leader development

Energy

Behaviors

Relationships

Values

Truth

Purpose

- Authentic leaders have clarity of **purpose**
- Authentic leaders are committed to living their core **values**
- Authentic leaders are disciplined in their **behaviors**
- Authentic leaders understand that **truth** is the lifeblood of growth
- Authentic leaders understand that managing **energy**, not time, is the key to personal growth and renewal
- Authentic leaders understand that growing **relationships** is what really matters

www.growingwinners.com

Byrd Baggett, CSP

Developing authentic leaders and passionately engaged teams since 1990

PRESENTATIONS

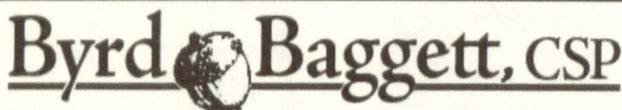

DARE TO GROW

How to build relationships
that last.

TRUE GROWTH
A New Philosophy of Leadership

How to become an authentic
leader who people want to follow.

NEW GROWTH

How to keep your business and
life green & growing.

LEGACY LEADING
The Power of Your Story

How to live a life that
really matters.

www.byrdbaggett.com   byrd@byrdbaggett.com   Phone: 251-610-7574

www.ingramcontent.com/pod-product-compliance
Lightning Source LLC
Chambersburg PA
CBHW022025170526
45157CB00003B/1357